Puffin Books

**Sky in the Pie**

'Waiter, there's a sky in my pie!'

Readers of this collection of poems by Roger McGough will discover that many intriguing dishes have been set before them to taste: some to choke with laughter about, some to chew very slowly. Brimming with vitality and humour and spiced with thoughtful observation, these poems will appeal to every young reader and are served up with the delicious accompaniment of Satoshi Kitamura's lively and highly original illustrations.

Roger McGough is one of today's most popular poets, having come to prominence in the 1960s as one of the Liverpool Poets. He spends his time writing, and earns his living reading his poems all over Britain and overseas in public performances and on the radio and television. He has written a number of plays and published many books for adults and children.

*Also by Roger McGough*

*Poetry*

YOU TELL ME: POEMS (*with Michael Rosen*)
NAILING THE SHADOW
PILLOW TALK
AN IMAGINARY MENAGERIE
MY DAD'S A FIRE-EATER
HELEN HIGHWATER
LUCKY: A BOOK OF POEMS
SKY IN THE PIE

*Fiction*

THE GREAT SMILE ROBBERY
THE STOWAWAYS

*For Older Readers*

STRICTLY PRIVATE
YOU AT THE BACK

Roger McGough

# Sky in the Pie

Illustrated by Satoshi Kitamura

Puffin Books

PUFFIN BOOKS

Published by the Penguin Group
Penguin Books Ltd, 27 Wrights Lane, London W8 5TZ, England
Penguin Books USA Inc., 375 Hudson Street, New York, New York 10014, USA
Penguin Books Australia Ltd, Ringwood, Victoria, Australia
Penguin Books Canada Ltd, 10 Alcorn Avenue, Toronto, Ontario, Canada M4V 3B2
Penguin Books (NZ) Ltd, 182–190 Wairau Road, Auckland 10, New Zealand

Penguin Books Ltd, Registered Offices: Harmondsworth, Middlesex, England

First published by Kestrel Books 1983
Published in Puffin Books 1985
10

Printed in England by Clays Ltd, St Ives plc
Set in Times Roman

*This one is for Finn, Tom and
as far ago as Nathan*

# Contents

## Sky in the Pie!

Waiter, there's a sky in my pie
Remove it at once if you please
You can keep your incredible sunsets
I ordered mincemeat and cheese

I can't stand nightingales singing
Or clouds all burnished with gold
The whispering breeze is disturbing the peas
And making my chips go all cold

I don't care if the chef is an artist
Whose canvases hang in the Tate
I want two veg. and puff pastry
Not the Universe heaped on my plate

OK I'll try just a spoonful
I suppose I've got nothing to lose
Mm . . . the colours quite tickle the palette
With a blend of delicate hues

The sun has a custardy flavour
And the clouds are as light as air
And the wind a chewier texture
(With a hint of cinnamon there?)

This sky is simply delicious
Why haven't I tried it before?
I can chew my way through to Eternity
And still have room left for more

Having acquired a taste for the Cosmos
I'll polish this sunset off soon
I can't wait to tuck into the night sky
Waiter! Please bring me the Moon!

## Mrs Moon

Mrs Moon
sitting up in the sky
little old lady
rock-a-bye
with a ball of fading light
and silvery needles
knitting the night

## Time-For-Bed

Time-For-Bed is a spoilsport
Every single night
When you're right
In the middle of something really interesting
In he charges
Large as a sore thumb.

Time-For-Bed
Eats impatient sandwiches
And wears bossy boots
(I sometimes think that grownups
must be in CAHOOTS)

# CAHOOTS?

## CAHOOTS?

Cahoots Cahoots
I'm in cahoots
spaghetti confetti
and caramel flutes

Cahoots Cahoots
back to the roots
micro–chip–butties
and para-graph-chutes.

## Tell Me Why?

Daddy will you tell me why
There are no battleships in the sky?
    The reason is apparently
    They only battle on the sea

Then will you tell me if you please
Why grandfather clocks cannot sneeze?
    The reason is, or so I'm told
    They're too stupid and too old

Will you explain once and for all
Why little Jack Horner fell off the wall?
    It wasn't him it was little Bo Peep
    Now be a good boy and go to sleep

Daddy will you tell me when
Little boys grow into men?
    Some never do that's why they fight
    Now kiss me, let me hold you tight

For in the morning I must go
To join my regiment and so
    For Queen and country bravely die
    Son, oh son, please tell me why?

# The Leader

I wanna be the leader
I wanna be the leader
Can I be the leader?
Can I? I can?
Promise? Promise?
Yippee, I'm the leader
I'm the leader

OK what shall we do?

## Bully Night

Bully night
I do not like
the company you keep
The burglars and the bogeymen
who slink
while others sleep

Bully night
I do not like
the noises that you make
The creaking and the shrieking
that keep me
fast awake.

Bully night
I do not like
the loneliness you bring
the loneliness you bring
The loneliness, the loneliness
the loneliness you bring,
the loneliness you bring
the loneliness, the

## PC Plod is on the Beat

PC Plod is on the beat
See him walking down the street
Everything is peaceful here
Criminals all live in fear
of PC Plod, PC Plod, PC Plod.

Mobsters, robbers, thieves and thugs
Long-haired traffickers of drugs
Men who live off sin and vice
Are hunted down and trapped like mice
by PC Plod, PC Plod, PC Plod.

When you're all tucked up tonight
Warm pyjamas sleeping tight
A supercop patrols the town
Making sure you're safe and sound
it's PC Plod, PC Plod, PC Plod.

A guardian angel of the law
Knows just what his truncheon's for
From behind our bedroom doors
Let's all give three hearty snores
for PC Plod, PC Plod, PC Plod.

## Zebra Crossing

There is a Lollipopman
At the zebra crossing
With lollipops
He is trying
To lure zebras across
He makes me cross.
I cross.

# Out of Sight

'Cheer up mate'
shouted the jolly roadsweeper
to the longfaced passerby
And bending down
lifted up a corner
of the tarmac
and swept away the dust.

## Eye Sore

I saw
a building
soar
into the sky

making
the sky's
eye
sore.

# The Writer of This Poem

The writer of this poem
Is taller than a tree
As keen as the North wind
As handsome as can be

As bold as a boxing-glove
As sharp as a nib
As strong as scaffolding
As tricky as a fib

As smooth as a lolly-ice
As quick as a lick
As clean as a chemist-shop
As clever as a

The writer of this poem
Never ceases to amaze
He's one in a million billion
(or so the poem says!)

## The New Poem (*for 18 words*)

New words
Should be used to being
Where they have not yet got.
So this is the poem.

This poem is the words,
So new, have yet
Not got used to being.
Where should they be?

This poem is so new
The words have not yet
Got used to being
Where they should be.

## The Poet's Garden

The garden is looking particularly all right at this time of the year. There are yellow things everywhere and sort of red bits in waving clumps. The lawn is as green as grass and studded with delicate little yellow and white studs. Flowers, I think they are called.

## The Poet Takes a Walk in the Country

The mist cleared for a moment
And as if a dull curtain
Had been lifted by unseen hands
The sun danced on to the stage.

Magical was the transformation.
The hills seemed literally
To glow with life. Golden bubbles
Of birdsong rose from the meadow.

Trees held out their arms
In exultation. Pure cosmic joy.
Mother Nature crying out:
'Look at me! Look at me!'

(The poet, however, was too hungover to notice).

## The Poet Inspired

7-30 on a pristine June morning
Sitting up in bed, pen in hand
The poet is ready to compose
The first poem of the day.

A subject? He thinks around
For something to write about.
Sheep. Counting sheep! Yes,
That would be a worthy challenge.

A poem about counting sheep.
Counting sheep. 1 – 2 – 3. Counting
Sheep – 4 – 5. Sheep. Count
6 – Sheep. Sheee . . . . z – z – z.

# Snow and Ice Poems

(i)    Our street is dead lazy
especially in winter.
Some mornings you wake up
and it's still lying there
saying nothing. Huddled
under its white counterpane.

But soon the lorries arrive
like angry mums,
pull back the blankets
and send it shivering
off to work.

(ii)    To
boggan?
or not
to boggan?
That is the question.

(iii)    Winter
morning.
Snowflakes
for breakfast.
The street
outside
quiet
as a
long
white
bandage.

(iv)    The time I like best
is 6 a.m.
and the snow is six inches deep

Which I'm yet to discover
'cos I'm under the cover
and fast, fast asleep.

# *Haiku*

Snowman in a field
listening to the raindrops
wishing him farewell

## The Snowman

Mother, while you were at the shops
and I was snoozing in my chair
I heard a tap at the window
saw a snowman standing there

He looked so cold and miserable
I almost could have cried
so I put the kettle on
and invited him inside

I made him a cup of cocoa
to warm the cockles of his nose
then he snuggled in front of the fire
for a cosy little doze

He lay there warm and smiling
softly counting sheep
I eavesdropped for a little while
then I too fell asleep

Seems he awoke and tiptoed out
exactly when I'm not too sure
it's a wonder you didn't see him
as you came in through the door

(oh, and by the way,
the kitten's made a puddle on the floor)

## *Pussy Pussy Puddle Cat*

Pussy pussy puddle cat
what do you think
you're playing at
making puddles
on the mat
chairs and tables
don't do that!

## *Your Friend the Sun*

Your friend the sun
came round to call
You kept him waiting
in the hall
And as the afternoon wore on
two – three – four
and he was gone

## Late Autumn Poem

birdless, and
almost bared,
Trees,
twigs chattering,
squeeze the last drops
out of the sun
and rub them
deep into parts
only trees know about.

## MARCH *ingorders*

Winter has been sacked
for negligence

It appears he left
the sun on all day

## Summer Days

I have a friend who is a back street
meteorologist. Amongst other things,
he told me that as hot air rises,
so in summer, the days get lighter.

# The Unincredible Hulk-in-law

Being the Incredible Hulk's
scrawny stepbrother ain't easy.
Sticky-fisted toddlers
pick fights with me
in misadventure playgrounds.

On beaches
seven-stone weaklings
kick sand in my eyes
vandalize my pies
and thrash me with candyfloss.

They all tell their friends
how they licked the Hulk . . .
(. . . well not the Hulk exactly,
but an incredibly unincredible relative).

Bullied by Brownies
mugged by nuns
without a doubt
the fun's gone out
of having a T.V. star in the family.

Think I'll marry
Wonderwoman's asthmatic second cousin
and start a commune in Arkansas
for out-of-work, weedy
super heroes-in-law.

## Quick on the Draw

He was so quickonthedraw
He fired twice
Had a haircut
A drink in the saloon
And rode out of town
Before the sheriff's hand
Hit the holster.

## Slow on the Drawl

'Howdy y'all'
said the Texan
(slow on the drawl)

# Harum Scarum

I am harum
I disturb the peace
I go around
saying boo to geese

I am scarum
I tell white lies
given half a chance
I would hurt flies

I am harum scarum
a one man gang
diddle dum darum
bang bang bang

## Cinema Poem

I like it when
They get shot in the head
And there's blood on the pillow
And blood on the bed

And it's good when
They get stabbed in the eye
And they scream and they take
A long time to die

And it all spurts out
All over the floor
And the audience shivers
And shouts for more

But I don't like it when they kiss.

## Is Violence on the Increase?

Hard to say really. Those who get mugged and beaten up regularly as clockwork oranges all agree that it is. But those of us who don't aren't too sure. The other day I went round to my local police station to put a similar question to the Superintendent. Unfortunately he had been vandalized on his way to work and was disable to answer.

## A Poem about Violence

If violence is what you want
Then this is the poem for you.
15 lines of action packed fury
Starring, the Fist, the Boot,
Even the Knife. No Guns.
I do not have a licence
For carrying guns in my poems.
Nevertheless there is plenty of
Screaming and swearing. Horrible.
Blood soaks through the page
Like an amazing image.

But what is the point of a
Poem about violence you ask?
The answer, I hope, will not be
Waiting outside to follow you home.

## Beatings

My father beats me up
Just like his father did
And grandad he was beaten
by greatgrandad as a kid

From generation to generation
A poisoned apple passed along
Domestic daily cruelty
No one thinking it was wrong.

And it was:

Not the cursing and the bruising
The frustration and the fear
A normal child can cope with that
It grows easier by the year

But the ignorance, believing
That the child is somehow owned
Property paid for
Violence condoned.

# *People I'd Rather Not Talk About*

\*\*\* is someone
I'd rather not talk about
\*\*\* is another

I don't care much for \*\*\* †
or \*\*\*, her little brother

It goes without saying
That I can't stand \*\*\* †

And I'd like to finish off with \*\*\*

† Those two rhyme

## Pets

Pets are a godsend to people who enjoy the company of
small animals. Cats, for example, are very popular.
As are dogs. We had a dog once called Rover, but he
died. So now we don't call him anything.

## The Pet

I asked my mum
If I could have a pet
'One day' she said,
'But not yet. Not yet.'

I was five then
And each year I tried
'Not yet, not yet'
Mum always replied

I'm ten now
And big for my age
And I've just built
A wooden cage

For now I've a pet
To put inside
Something belonging
To someone who died

He keeps me company
When I feel sad
He's my pet slipper
And I call him 'Dad'.

## Bring Back the Cat

*Bring back the cat*
*Bring back the cat*
*My little girl say*
*Bring back the cat*

*Bring back the cat*
*Bring back the cat*
*My little girl*
*She really like that*

My little girl she four in May
Got a pet kitten, it black and grey
Playing in the garden just the other day
Kitten went missing, must have gone astray
(Unless some kittennapper took her away)

Went right down to the RSPCA
Told me not to worry, it would be OK
Nothing more to do 'cept hope and pray
Maybe he bring it back some day
That why my little girl she say:

*Bring back the cat*
*Bring back the cat*
*My little girl say*
*Bring back the cat*

*Bring back the cat*
*Bring back the cat*
*My little girl she*
*Really like that*

# Friendship Poems

(i)    There's good mates and bad mates
        'Sorry to keep you waiting' mates
    Cheap skates and wet mates
        The ones you end up hating mates
    Hard mates and fighting mates
        Witty and exciting mates
    Mates you want to hug
        And mates you want to clout
    Ones that get you into trouble
        And ones that get you out.

(ii)    Two's company
    One's lonely.

(iii)    I'm a fish out of water
    I'm two left feet
    On my own and lonely
    I'm incomplete

    I'm boots without laces
    I'm jeans without the zip
    I'm lost, I'm a zombie
    I'm a dislocated hip.

(iv)    When you're young
    Love sometimes confuses
    It clouds the brain
    And blows the fuses
    How often during those tender years
    You just can't see the wood for the tears.

## Life on Mars

Is there life on Mars? Yes, there is. I know because my Auntie Pat lived there for over three years. She went in October 1969 and worked as a garage pump attendant for a couple of months, before getting a good job in a shipping office. She reckoned it was much the same as anywhere else. During her stay she hitchhiked all over the planet, earning her keep as a waitress or chambermaid. She's got some really fantastic stories about Martians. Yes, there certainly is life on Mars. You ask my Auntie Pat.

## Dancin'

When I'm dancin'
I forget everythin'
I become the music
The band takes me over.
I sing
I'm the singer
I play the riffs
I'm the lead guitar
ba bum bum
I'm the bass
          But most of all
I'm the drummer
The drums
I'm the drums
I'm drums on legs
The drums
Drums on legs
The drums
Drums on legs
The drums
Drums on legs
The drums
Drums on legs
The beat
The beat takes me over.

When the music
stops
It's so quiet
I can hear myself
sweatin'.

## Man the Musicmaker

In the beginning was the word
the stillborn silence broken
word followed word
and man's first song was spoken

Then the air filled with sounds
wind and sea and bird
man listened in amazement
then copied what he heard

The wind plucked the strings of the forest
whistled through canyon and plain
thunder beat drums in the nightsky
as lightning crashed cymbals in rain

In the beginning was the word
the stillborn silence broken
word followed word
and man's first song was spoken

Then the air filled with music
flute and drum and lyre
for Man the Musicmaker
had set his soul on fire.

## Classical Records

The greatest classical record must be, either
Beethoven's leap over three baby grands at a 21st party
in Zurich, or J. S. Bach's eating of 55 fried
frankfurters at a frankfurter festival in Frankfurt.

Mozart, of course, claims to have run the 100 metres in
9.8 seconds when he was seven years old. But he was
always saying things like that. Wrote good tunes but
he was a right bighead.

## Javelin Catching

I see that javelin catching is becoming increasingly popular on the lunatic fringe at sporting circles. This appals me. The idea of grown men (and women) spending their Saturday afternoons engaged in such blood-letting must say something for the sorry state of Britain in the eighties. The practice, apparently, is that the contestants wear vests with targets printed on, and the sport (*my italics*) consists of trying to impale oneself on a javelin thrown from one hundred metres. What next I ask myself – hurdling over high voltage electric wires? – pole vaulting into a cage of lions? Heading the shot?

# Cup-Final

T. O'Day

W. E. March        T. O. G. Lory

J. Usty        O. Uwait        N. See

G. O'Dow
A. Day        W. Ewill                N. Infa        H. I. Story


Young        N. Fast                M. O'Reskill  I. T. Sreally
W. Egot

A. L. L. Sewnup    W. E. Rethel    A. D. S. Whollrun

A. Round        W. Embley

W. I. Thecup

## My Week

My week started on MONDAY and
then went into TUESDAY. Before
I knew where I was it was WEDNESDAY
with THURSDAY following soon after.
FRIDAY was not far behind, when lo and
behold, it was SATURDAY. My week ended
on SUNDAY.

## A Bowl of Fruit

In the wooden bowl
(wood coloured) are 4 apples,
3 pears and an orange.
Can you see them?

What colour are the pears?
Green? Correct. (Although
they might have been yellow.)

The apples? Wrong.
3 green and one red.

The orange? Of course,
orange. Secure in the sense
of its own glowing identity
the Lord of the Bowl
reigns over the room.
Cezanne of citrus.
Plump Picasso of peel.

## The cabbage is a funny veg.

The cabbage is a funny veg.
All crisp, and green, and brainy.
I sometimes wear one on my head
When it's cold and rainy.

## My Week

This week my week started on THURSDAY then went straight into TUESDAY. SUNDAY followed looking a trifle puzzled and no wonder because WEDNESDAY came next. MONDAY tottered in leading SATURDAY by the morning. FRIDAY surrendered and the week was up.

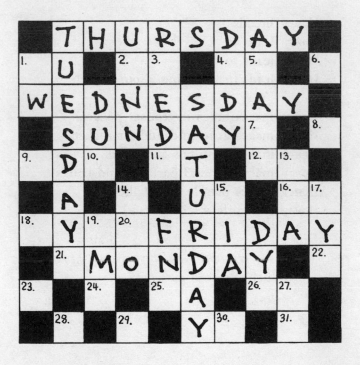

## Money moans

*Money* I haven't got enough
*Money* I'll never have enough
*Money* is what I want, I want
*Money* so that I don't have to worry about

*Money* When you have lots of
*Money* you can make lots more
*Money* by doing nothing but letting your
*Money* work for you by making

*Money* breeds
*Money* leads to
*Money* leads to
*Money* leads to worrying about

*Money* makes holes in trouser pockets
*Money* makes guns and nuclear rockets
*Money* makes hospitals and tanks
*Money* makes funeral parlours and banks
*Money* makes people go off the rails
*Money* fills coffers, coffins and jails

I lie awake at night
Worrying about          *money*
A taxperson somewhere
Spends all the days
Making lots of          *money*
Finding new ways
To keep me awake at night
Worrying about          *money*

Mone mone money
Ail I do is moan
about money.

## Potato Clock

A potato clock, a potato clock
   Has anybody got a potato clock?
A potato clock, a potato clock
   Oh where can I find a potato clock?

I went down to London the other day
Found myself a job with a lot of pay
Carrying bricks on a building site
From early in the morning till late at night

No one here works as hard as me
I never even break for a cup of tea
My only weakness, my only crime
Is that I can never get to work on time

A potato clock, a potato clock
   Has anybody got a potato clock?
A potato clock, a potato clock
   Oh where can I find a potato clock?

I arrived this morning half an hour late
The foreman came up in a terrible state
'You've got a good job, but you'll lose it, cock,
If you don't get up at eight o'clock.'

Up at eight o'clock, up at eight o'clock
   Has anybody got up at eight o'clock?
Up at eight o'clock, up at eight o'clock
   Oh where can I find up at eight o'clock?

## Easy Money

Guess how old I am?
I bet you can't.
I bet you.
Go on guess.
Have a guess.

Wrong!
Have another.

Wrong!
Have another

Wrong again!
Do you give in?

Seven years four months two weeks
five days three hours fifteen
minutes forty-eight seconds!
That's 20p you owe me.

## My Week

MONDAY – wrote novel, two TV plays and a book of light verse. TUESDAY – got up early, had light breakfast (two 50 watt bulbs), swam channel. Back in time to watch Coronation Street. WEDNESDAY – organized and took part in four armed robberies, in Birmingham area. Came home with £250,000. THURSDAY laid low – played with the kids. Wrote second novel. FRIDAY – blackmailed local alderman at lunchtime, went to PTA meeting at night. SATURDAY – sprang two mates from Strangeways. Watched Match of the Day.
SUNDAY – two mates came over for dinner. Roast lamb, carrots and turnips, jacket potatoes. Police raid during rice pudding – went quietly.

## Clank

Yesterday at dinner hour
while I was eating fish
I thought about
the fishermen
and made a little wish
I wish the fish
were silver
to make the fishtanks
clank
which fish
the then rich fishermen
could put in the
Dogger bank
(before they sank)
                    thank you

## *Whale Poems*

(i)   whales
are floating cathedrals
let us rejoice

cavorting mansions
of joy
let us give thanks

divine temples
of the deep
we praise thee


(ii)   whaleluja!

(iii)   whalemeat again
(don't know where
don't know when

but I know)
whalemeat again
(some sunny day)

(iv)   in the scheme
of things
oceanic
the whale is titanic

in the
pecking order
maritime
e l e p h a n t i n e

(v)   whale:
      my bull

      ocean:
      my corrida

      oilskin:
      my suit of lights

      harpoon:
      my sword of truth

      death:
      my fat purse.

## Friends of the Earth

Ecology Jim was a Friend of the Earth.
But the earth was no friend of Jim.
When living he covered all of it
Now it covers all of him.

## Yellow Poem

Each evening I eat lots of bread
with lots of yellow butter.
Enjoy my yellow omelette
with a little yellow cheese.

And before I make my yellow bed
in my tidy yellow room
I thank the Lord for yellowness
on my little yellow knees.

(Q. Why were your knees yellow?
A. Because I'd been kneeling in custard.)

## No More Ferries

*No more ferries*
*No river trips*
*No more dreams*
*on little ships*

Then how will little boys
Run away to sea
Have a day's adventure
And get home in time for tea?

Then how will lovers
Promenading hand in hand
Take a slow boat to Seacombe
And never sight land?

*No more ferries*
*No river trips*
*No more dreams*
*on little ships*

Then how will husbands
Who promised the wife a world cruise
Go below with a takeaway Chinese
And a couple of bottles of booze?

Then how will old men
Who know the oceans well
Relive salty memories
On the Mersey's homely swell?

*No more ferries*
*No river trips*
*No more dreams*
*on little ships*

**No more dreams on little ships.**

# Gone are the Liners

Gone are the liners
The 'Reina del Mars'
The P. & O.s
And the C.P.R.s

Gone are the liners
The pride of Cunard
Now ghost-ridden hulks
In the knacker's yard

Gone are the liners
The glories of old
Now seagulls redundant
Sign on at the dole

## Fire Guard

My wife bought a fire guard for the living room.
Seems a nice sort of chap.

---

## Bank Holidays

This year, why not take your holidays in a bank?
A fortnight in Barclays, Clacton, or a long weekend
at the Nat. West. in Harrogate might be just the
tonic. Meet interesting cashiers, witness the thrills and
spills of accountancy. And remember, you don't need a
passport to spend the day at a foreign exchange
counter. Full details from your local detailer.

---

## Valentine Poem

If I were a poet
I'd write poems for you.
If I were a musician,
Music too.
But as I'm only an average man
I give you my love
As best what I can.

If I were a sculptor
I'd sculpt you in stone.
An osteopath,
Work myself to the bone.
But as I'm just a man in the street
I give you my love,
Lay my heart at your feet

*(ugh!)*

If I were an orator
I'd make pretty speeches.
An oil tanker,
Break up on your beaches.
But as I'm just an ordinary Joe
I send you my love,
As best what I know.

## The Body

The Body is composed of fatty tissues, blood, water,
cells and hairy parts not to mention. It is a marvellous
piece of biological engineering. Blood goes round and
stuff comes out and we can play tennis and write
philosophical treatises. Yes, I wouldn't be seen dead in
the street without one.

# *Hoiku*

(Hawick, pronounced Hoik, is a little town in Scotland)

unless I'm on strawick
(or off sawick) I lawick to bawick
to my wawick at Hawick

# *A, A, B, B,*

Trying to write without a rhyme
Gets more difficult all the time
I wish that I could now reverse
This facility in my verse.

# *Why do sheep*

Why do sheep
have curly coats?

To keep the wind
out of their froats

# Today's Recipe – Book Soup

Choose a book with plenty of fat on it. Your local
bookseller will be happy to advise you on this.
He'll probably suggest a dictionary or a nice juicy
biography or even an anthology which is a very
popular cut at the moment. Mash the book into a pulp,
add some bacon rind, a dash of poetry criticism
and season to taste. Heat in a low oven
(preferably under eighteen inches) until thickened.
Serve hot with deep fried crispy bookworms.

## *I'm a grown man now*

I'm a grown man now
Don't easily scare
(if you don't believe me
ask my teddy bear).

## A Poem Just for Me

Where am I now when I need me
Suddenly where have I gone
I'm so alone here without me
Tell me please what have I done?

Once I did most things together
I went for walks hand in hand
I shared my life so completely
I met my every demand.

Tell me I'll come back tomorrow
I'll keep my arms open wide
Tell me that I'll never leave me
My place is here at my side.

Maybe I've simply mislaid me
Like an umbrella or key
So until the day that I come my way
Here is a poem just for me.

# Index of First Lines